I AM WHO LOVES THE PROPHETS

An Exile Devotional

I AM
WHO LOVES THE
PROPHETS

An Exile Devotional

Marc H. Ellis

WIPF & STOCK · Eugene, Oregon

Wipf and Stock Publishers
199 W 8th Ave, Suite 3
Eugene, OR 97401

I Am Who Loves the Prophets
An Exile Devotional
By Ellis, Marc H.
Copyright © 2020 by Ellis, Marc H. All rights reserved.
Softcover ISBN-13: 978-1-6667-5042-3
Hardcover ISBN-13: 978-1-6667-5043-0
eBook ISBN-13: 978-1-6667-5044-7
Publication date 6/13/2022
Previously published by Claretian Communications Foundation, Inc., 2020

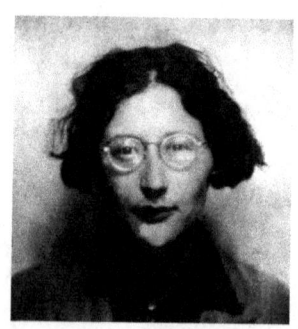

First you said to me at the beginning of our relationship some words that went to the bottom of my soul. You said: 'Be very careful, because if you should pass over something very important through your own fault it would be a pity.'

~ Simone Weil

Acknowledgments

A special thanks to Keren Batiyov and Coy Dionco for their editorial assistance and support in helping to bring this devotional into existence; to my children, Aaron and Isaiah, for their loving presence in my life; and to my fellow beach-walker's community who no doubt wondered what my sunrise writing was all about.

Preface

A Pentecostal Christian once asked me, and then again, as a Jew, both times in a gentle way: 'Why not write a devotional?'

My first 'no' hardly deterred him. My second – 'I'll think about it' – wasn't strong enough. One day I sat down and began.

Little of religion's traditional language ever appealed to me. Any devotional I write will hardly match the genre's expectation.

As a child I was suspicious of God-talk though, as is evident in my devotions, I embraced parts of my tradition at the deepest levels of my being.

As a student at university in the 1970s, I encountered theology after the Holocaust. As Jews, what can we say about God after the Holocaust? In the 1980s, I encountered Palestinians. As Jews, what can we say about God in a time when our empowerment oppresses another people?

Finding my voice after the Holocaust and after what Israel has done and is doing to the Palestinian people was easy for me. Once I witnessed the oppression on the ground in Israel-Palestine, I never looked back. Yet speaking the truth to my people, performing the prophetic in our time, has consequences. Exile it was. Exile it is.

When I realized my exile was permanent I was confronted with another series of questions. Can I be in exile, as a Jew, without God? How can I speak about God in exile in an unredeemed world? How can I articulate God after the Holocaust and the oppression that fills our world?

Thus I offer my devotional, in the only way I can, as a meditation of sorts and with words I know are hardly adequate. I offer my devotional for others who might find it of use for their own faith journey or, better, spur them to imagine their own devotional.

Jews, Christians and Muslims, with other religions, too, are in similar situations of disappointment and hope. If we worship the same God, can we read and benefit from each other's devotionals?

Few will call my meditations inspirational. In my experience devotion is hardly such, at least not as we think of inspiration today.

From the beginning, Jews have shied away from naming God, using stand-ins, surrogates and proxies like Elohim and Adonai – God and Lord. In the Bible, if God has a name it was either lost in Israel's early history or never fully known. This inability to name God has co-existed with the sense that naming God limits God. Limiting God is a form of idolatry.

Nonetheless, the Biblical name for God, a series of four letters, YHWH, known as the tetragrammaton, has been variously translated into different forms: I AM THAT I AM or I AM WHO WILL BE. As my exile deepens I AM WHO LOVES THE PROPHETS has become my way of addressing God.

My name for God came to me one day. Just like that. I cannot explain where it came from.

Addressing God by name signals such a sea-change in my spiritual life that it surprises others when they hear me address God in this manner. God's name came to me by surprise. Addressing God is my response to life as it is.

Does this mean I know God because I have fashioned a name for God that makes sense for my journey? Or that the questions about God that I have had for so long have now been answered? Not in the least.

My devotional has a different feel to it than the usual ones. Praise and encouragement are in short supply. That is, unless one views living the question of God as honestly as possible to be a form of praise and encouragement.

Exile, forced or chosen, is not for the faint of heart. Neither is my devotional.

Except for my title, I do not use my name for God in this devotional. I do not name God at all. Perhaps it is best to keep God unnamed after all. Or rather, named and unnamed.

The Name of All Names remains open to you, the reader, or might become open once again to all of us. As it was in the beginning?

Another devotional warning – I do not offer quotes from Scripture, though I do allude to my favorite prophets, Ezekiel and Elijah. I do cite the words of unexpected devotional contributors, Franz Kafka, the Jewish novelist, Albert Camus, the French agnostic, and Samuel Beckett, the Irish playwright of abject despair.

More on the beaten path, I refer to the writing of the Catholic monk, Thomas Merton. I think with the Protestant conspirator against Hitler, Dietrich Bonhoeffer and hope with the French Jewish-Christian, Simone Weil. I explore the provocative Buddhist spirituality of Milarepa and Shunryu Suzuki and search for truth with the feminist Jewish poet, Adrienne Rich. I struggle with the enigmatic theologian of God, among freedom fighters, by way of the Catholic priest, Joan Casañas.

My guides are from different religions and from different parts of the world. The meaning of what it means to be Jewish today cannot be found only among Jews. Is this so different from the search for what it means to be Christian or Muslim? We need each other.

Though my devotional entries are undated, my devotional path leads to the holy days of Easter and Passover. So without appealing to scripture or God, in my devotional I remain within the religious calendar.

Even though exiles and the prophets are on their own, we have a tradition that can be referenced as a guide. Even if, on occasion, our traditions are cause for rebellion.

Being on our own, with our particular histories, we can begin again.

Forgive me. I cannot start at your beginning.

My prayer cupboard has been empty for most of my life. In my youth I didn't bow my head. I didn't say 'God.' As a child, I recited prayers at bedtime yet, even as an adult, I never thought of a personal God. Until my exile arrived and darkness was around every corner.

I still find it difficult to be near those who know who God is. As difficult as it is to be close to those who know who God isn't.

God is. God isn't. The dichotomy I knew. *Before.*

The prophetic is a different story. I have always been drawn to the prophetic. Without knowing why.

As a child, 'it' was already there. Later I came to know 'it' as the prophetic. I was relieved. 'It' had a proper name.

I wasn't raised on the Bible. The Bible came later.

Over the years, I have become more articulate about the prophetic and the Bible. I had to. I couldn't make it without God in exile.

My exile continues unabated. For many of us, there is no exile end in sight.

Naming our journey's interior, even when the time is late. Strange, naming what we need for the journey is always, also, right on time.

◆•◆•◆•◆

I live near the beach. Each morning I awaken for a sunrise walk. My sunrise walk ahead, I lie in bed thinking of my lack of devotion. My difficulty saying 'God.'

With my children I said 'God.' After my oldest son, Aaron, was born, we started celebrating Shabbat. I created a morning prayer from different sources. We recited this prayer together before he and later his younger brother, Isaiah, went off to school.

My boys are now grown. We recite our prayer when they arrive for a visit. And when they leave. They lead. I listen.

I pray when I am alone. But I miss that prayer together. I do.

◆•◆•◆•◆

Dear God,

Thank you for awakening me to this new day
Making me a Jew
Calling me to be free
And forming me in the Divine Image.

Help me to be awake
To the wonders that surround us
Alive to beauty and love
Aware that all being is precious
And that we walk on Holy Ground wherever we go.

Shema Israel Adonai Eloheinu Adonai Echad.

Hear, O Israel, the Lord our God, the Lord is One.

Hear O Israel.

The martyr's prayer, said so many times in different ages by Jews on the run, under assault, about to die, is also the great affirmation of the oneness of God.

The *Shema* affirms God's presence to the people Israel. And beyond.

In the morning, I send my children on their way. With God's blessing. The prayer reminds them of their beginning. Their end.

When I led our prayer, and now when the boys do, I affirm the God I am unsure of. I am in mourning, too.

Am I mourning the God that was with us and is no longer, who called us to challenge the powers that be and to embrace a special destiny for ourselves and the world?

I experience the end of Jewish life in the Holocaust. I experience the debasement of Jewish life in our oppression of another people.

Precious life is being dishonored everywhere. Prayer cannot stop the oppression.

Does God hear my mournful prayer?

After Aaron was born, I attended a synagogue where the rabbi was honest and committed to social justice. I recited the synagogue prayers, though with some reluctance. Public prayer carries a double warning for me. How can words crafted by others speak to each individual in community?

As I pray, every word became a question. Are Jews really chosen? Is God standing by us as history unfolds?

I think of my (un)belief. Over time I decided to move beyond the surface meaning of words. Now, I rest more easily in the rhythm of prayer. In the poetry of prayer. Sometimes.

Lost in the rhythm and poetry of prayer, we finish. I bless the Shabbat lights. Bread is eaten. On to the wine.

———◆•◆•◆•◆———

My sunrise walk starts before the sun rises. Then, the sky's colors are changing and most vivid.

Today's sky is unspectacular and wonderful nonetheless. Long horizontal clouds in dark shades of blue, framed by a light gray sky. Though the tide is low, the ocean is loud. So loud I hear it blocks away as I approach.

Have I forgotten the God I did not know? Or has God always been with me? A name I did not know?

The sun rises. I wonder if the prophetic within me is God.

———◆•◆•◆•◆———

Exile does this to us.

At times we forget where we began. We begin again. Words we knew are lost. We invent new words to fit our exile experience. Words name our reality. Then they exist on their own.

Like covenant. Promised Land. Prophet. Ancient. New.

I sit on a long wooden walkway that serves as a bridge to the ocean. The bridge has a wooden bench and an open canopy. I call it my Chapel of Love.

I walked this beach when, as a child, my parents took the family on vacation. Now, living here, I walk the beach daily. I only noticed this canopied bridge a year or so ago. Now I sit watching the sky change and sunrise arrive.

My Chapel of Love is a touchstone. A place of refuge. Where I find the God I have difficulty naming.

Now it is hard for me to remember the time before I discovered my place of refuge.

This morning I think of my journey. What has died within me? What has been reborn?

◆·◆·◆·◆

Lost and found. Naming both. Thinking backwards. Thinking ahead.

In exile it is hard to remain in the present.

We cannot relive our before. *After* is the present to come.

Exile is now. With and without God.

Even the prophetic has to rest. Prophetic activism without reflection is another flight. Exile within exile.

Traveling. Seeking justice everywhere. The long plane rides. Cheap hotels. People's homes. Hospitality on the run. On foreign shores.

Prophetic ramblings. To what purpose? Most of the world is the same or worse when I arrive at my destination. When departing, I am the same or worse. Yet somehow changed.

That world within me. The trauma of suffering.

The trauma of the prophetic. Shall I banish my trauma or hold it high for all to see? For the most part, my trauma is well hidden. Deep waters.

I think of trauma as if time is running out. So many stories to tell. They aren't mine alone.

Our stories.

Journeys coming to a close. Journeys just beginning. Once in a while our paths cross. We meet in the middle.

As we awake and when we lie down to sleep, Jews are instructed to pray. To keep our anxiety at bay? The night is not our end. Day dawns.

As I embark on my sunrise walks, I see my neighbor's television screen alight. Wide screen. Wider still. Morning ritual. Deflection?

In exile, distractions are necessary. Distractions can overwhelm us. Is forgetfulness bliss?

If we pay attention, exile is a teachable moment. If we want to learn. If we are open to the pain that exile learning brings.

Real teachers are on the run from the powers that be. Real students will be too.

Exile as a university. Homeless bound.

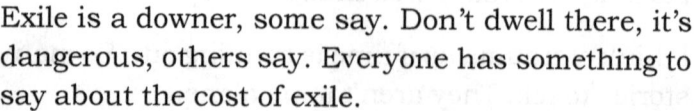

Exile is a downer, some say. Don't dwell there, it's dangerous, others say. Everyone has something to say about the cost of exile.

Exile is costly. Exiles search for solid footing. Trying to avoid exile's slippery slope.

Romanticizing exile is foolish. Taking exile on for sympathy is foolhardy. If the exile is real let it flow.

The tradition of exile is often romanticized. Exile isn't for the faint of heart. Exile is the real deal.

Exile's connection with the prophetic is ancient. One without the other is impossible. In our exalted modernity, exile and the prophetic are like visitors from another planet.

Expressing the pain of exile is ancient, too. So is the hope of exile. Effusive colors.

Practicing exile is the Jewish (and non-Jewish) thing to do. Developing that practice and sharing it with other exiles in need. Challenging.

If I wasn't in exile, where would I be? If I wasn't in exile, who would I be?

Exiles ask these questions.

Corruption surrounds us. We have to participate at some level just to get by. The academy, business, government, churches, mosques and synagogues are filled with corruption. The prophetic resides within all of these institutions but is deflected and diverted.

The prophetic is entangled. As is exile.

Perfection eludes us. Should perfection be sought?

Though we live in an imperfect world filled with imperfect beings, there are limits. There are places we cannot venture beyond. Lines we dare not cross.

Even if once we didn't cross red lines. There comes a moment – we have to take a stand.

Taking stands, we find our center. Our reason. Life.

Reading the letters of Samuel Beckett, the playwright who wrote *Waiting for Godot*. The difference between Beckett's desperate plays and his compassionate life is significant. Others notice this, too. Beckett was an enigma.

Beckett's plays are bleak. *Waiting for Godot* was only the tip of Beckett's despair.

Yet Beckett's letters are filled with compassion for others. As he writes of life without rescue, Beckett offers struggling playwrights advice and money. Beckett offers condolences for the sick he knows and visits old friends who are unknown in the literary world. He protests censorship and aids those hit hard for their practice of justice. Beckett gardens.

Yet Beckett was never able to translate his compassion for others into another way of looking at the world. It is difficult to argue with Beckett's sense of despair. His vision of hopeless hope. God isn't a cheerleader.

I am struck by Beckett's honesty and struggle. I am struck by his obstinacy. Beckett wasn't going to move in another direction, no matter what.

Exile presents a similar challenge. Pie in the sky isn't going to move the exile ball down the field. Nor is dwelling on the misgivings of life. There is a difference between reflecting on exile and being stuck there.

Being stuck in exile is no place to be. The way forward?

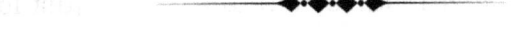

Try new things, they say. Reinvent yourself. Advice is cheap. Endless.

This morning I resolve to move deeper into the solitude within me. Instead of running from the world. Take a different approach.

Find solace in exile. Beauty. Hold the moment of dispossession in one hand and the moment of liberation in the other.

Exile happened, liberation hasn't. Thinking in a linear way. But dispossession is rarely a singular moment affair. Liberation won't be a one moment affair either.

I think of dispossession and liberation as entwined. A lifelong dance. One predominates at times, the other at other times. Neither completes the other. Or halts the dance.

Without thinking resurrection. Of body or soul. As both are usually discussed.

Think Archbishop Oscar Romero. He hoped to be resurrected in the history of the Salvadoran people. Think Martin Luther King. Though both knew they wouldn't reach the Promised Land, they already had a taste of glory in the movement of their people.

I experience their resurrection talk. Was it just for them?

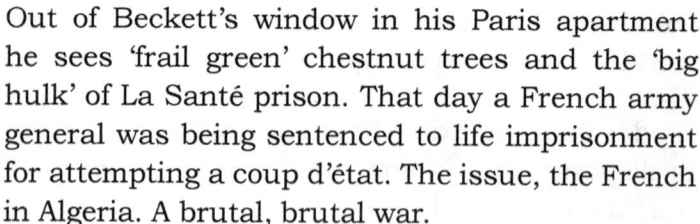

Out of Beckett's window in his Paris apartment he sees 'frail green' chestnut trees and the 'big hulk' of La Santé prison. That day a French army general was being sentenced to life imprisonment for attempting a coup d'état. The issue, the French in Algeria. A brutal, brutal war.

Beckett's writing desk overlooked what's left of nature in cities, and a prison, hallmark of state power. Wars without end, retreating nature and state power were contested then. They are contested now.

The exile's writing desk today is in that same orbit. Defending what is left of nature. Challenging state power. Victories are few and far between.

Exile is a prison. The prophetic is, too. Exile and the prophetic know each other well. On the field of battle.

I read a Jewish author who wants to escape his Jewish identity. He refers to his Jewishness as a prison. My thought is different. True, you cannot escape Jewishness. The world has marked you. So has God. Between these markings lay our freedom.

Our constraint as our freedom?

It isn't only Jewish. The place we want to escape is the place of our grounding. In the cauldron, we go forth into the world engraved.

'Into the path you are hurled,' Bob Dylan sings.

---◆·◆·◆---

The prophetic shadows us. Won't let us go. We don't want the prophetic. Should we?

The prophetic as burden. Prison time. Exile, too. Solitary confinement. I hear the exile door close behind me. Have you?

Especially when lauded as a prophet. Death sentence. Still, I have never experienced the prophetic as a burden. The betrayal cannot be laid at the feet of the prophetic.

The prophetic in our lives is that unerring sensibility. The thread that takes us through life. With meaning. And after the tumult, the prophetic is the still point. Honed.

Without the prophetic we lose our balance. The balance that rights what the world does with the prophetic. Without the prophetic there is no meaning in life.

The prophetic creates the ultimate instability in history and in our lives. Such instability is our authentic stability. Is this because the prophetic was given by an unstable God?

───────◆·◆·◆───────

Yes, the God of the Hebrew Bible. An unstable character!

Imagine that God, my God, our God, chooses a nothing of a people. Their destiny? To create a just society.

Imagine that God, my God, our God, sends unstable prophets to chastise a people whose very stability is the prophetic.

A mouthful for a devotional moment. But think. Those who believe in the Hebrew God have at their center a stability that worldly-wise seems a contradiction in terms. If that was not enough, that God, my God, our God, continuously sends unstable messengers to decry the worldly stability that causes the prophets trouble without end.

Pray for that instability. As if our lives depend on it. Even as we live our exile lives. Counterintuitive, at the very least. If we are honest.

More. Be grateful for the uprootings that frame our life. Be grateful for the uprootings to come.

Morning. Thinking of being bound. And being free.

My morning prayer comes back to me. Is thinking my prayer, praying?

I feel bound and unfree. I feel free and unbound.

Have I ever truly been unbound? Have I ever been truly free?

Thanking God for binding me. For making me free.

Peculiar gratitude.

I had it wrong yesterday. Start again.

In prayer, I thank God for binding me. For making me a Jew. But God doesn't make me free. In prayer, God calls me to be free.

What is that calling? Content? Method? God's choosing cannot be like the schoolyard I played in as a child. 'Hey Ellis!'

Being bound. As a Jew. Does God point as we go by, singling some out for this religion and others for another?

Being called out. Designation: *Jew*. Thus a calling. To be free.

The freedom to be for self. The freedom to be for others.

Thanking God for awakening me to this new day. For the first time in a long time I said this aloud. Alone on the beach.

My sunrise walks saved me. As my exile deepened. Each morning a new day.

Waking up at different times of the night, often with great anxiety, isn't easy. I do not thank God for awakening me. In my exile night.

This new day. The evangelical first day of the rest of my life? I don't want to go there. Even if 'there' holds a truth?

Adrienne Rich, the late poet: 'Often such truth comes by accident, or from strangers.'

Another prayer to be said upon awakening?

◆•◆•◆•◆

By accident. From strangers. Truth comes. From? Truth, capital 'T'?

We look for Truth. Career. Calling. Future. Do we look in all the wrong places?

Exiles are careful of truth that comes by accident or from strangers. Since what comes our way is often wrapped in a fitful disguise. Doors that close behind us come by accident and from strangers, too. The door opening before us is often fraught.

Exiles walk on dangerous ground. To the Other who is bound and unfree by the powers that be. Is this ground holy?

Be careful with what you are called to be. Doors open and close. Sometimes the closed door remains closed. Forever.

Exile doors. Swing open. Swing shut.

When one door closes, another door opens. Too simple?

Whatever doesn't kill you, makes you stronger. Really?

God is with you in your struggle. Certain?

Thanking God for forming me in the Divine Image. Meaning?

So many clichés on the exile road.

Boatloads of self-help for exiles. Exiles Anonymous.

Needed: A thirteenth step.

Exiles Anonymous. Meeting all over the world.

We are alone. We are together. Both. At the same time.

The solitude we live is a burden. A warning. A gift.

Solitude is a fine line journey. Having been stuck there at times. Having been free there at times. Having shared solitude on occasion.

The solitude that is also a solidarity.

Solitude of the monk. The solitude of the heart. The solitude of the prophet. The solidarity of each.

The solitude without beginning or end.

Can we say the same for solidarity?

Some years ago my oldest son, Aaron, hung out with a group of punk Christians traveling through the city where I was teaching. Through them he became aware of a punk Christian band, The Psalters. Aaron gave their CD to me as a gift. I thanked him but doubted I would like it. I put the CD away for a rainy day.

Aaron isn't a stranger. He knows me well. He gifted me a truth I needed.

So when the rainy day came, I listened. It was strange at first, a Christian message of some sorts, but dark. Ambiguous. The beat was strong, irregular. I hadn't heard music like this before. I haven't since.

One song became an anthem for me. I played it over and over again. When I become stuck, I listen again.

The song begins with these words, also the song's refrain, the first four lines ascribed to an anonymous Jewish concentration camp inmate during World War II:

> I believe in the sun, though it is late to rise, late to rise
> I believe in love, though it is absent, I cannot give it or feel it
> I believe in God, though He is silent, I cannot hear Him I cannot but
> I will dream the impossible dream over lies over lies over lies
>
> I have eyes I have eyes I have eyes
> I will dream the impossible dream over lies

I am startled by the song's message. If a message can be discerned. One hardly believes in the sun. At least Christians don't. Is the sun ever late to rise? Believing in love in its absence as a hope is one thing. Being unable to give or feel love is another. Can I believe in a God who is silent? Is it my fault I rarely hear God?

The Psalters insist on dreaming the impossible dream. They see with their own eyes the choice before us. The impossible dream. Hope over corruption and lies.

'I have eyes I have eyes I have eyes' – the words keep coming – the beat is relentless. As The Psalters sing loudly over a driving beat, it isn't clear which will win out. Doubt is a challenge rather than an end to their belief. Belief is within doubt. Is belief, eyes wide open?

The exile experiences lies as a blunt force trauma. ER daily.

Does 'seeing' disarm lies? Exiles wonder.

What the prophets see in every age. What I have seen on my minor stage.

The world as it is. Unredeemed. No theology or spirituality can tell me different. I have eyes. We have eyes.

Worshipping God in an unredeemed world? The message of the prophets writ large in the vernacular: 'Injustice, then do not come to Me. Don't even think about it!'

So many of our Jewish prophets today want nothing to do with God. They think – they know? – that any God-appeal in an unredeemed world dodges the prophetic bullet.

Disagree? Liturgy and creeds, they are the death knell for the prophetic. 'Lord, I am not worthy!'

I still can't make it without God. Without making any claims on God's behalf.

Sunset. The colors too beautiful to be true. Good sleeping weather tonight. Windows wide open.

Falling asleep, my anxiety recedes. Then up in the middle of the night thinking of the broken places within me. The broken places of others. The broken places that have been hurled my way. The broken places I have caused.

Many endings. The endings that are natural. Watching out for the unnatural endings. Economic and political state power are out there. They come inside, too.

Thanking God for setting us apart as a people. On Shabbat that prayer runs through my mind. Thank God for setting me apart, too?

Apart. In the middle of the night. Different feeling than at the Shabbat table.

Isaiah: 'Here I am. Send me.'

The psychedelic prophet, Ezekiel. God commanding

him to eat the text of his doom. He does. Surprise, surprise, the text tastes sweet, just like honey.

The sweetness of exile. Rarely felt in the middle of the night.

All things must pass away. Beware of darkness. George Harrison's musings via the ancient traditions of Buddhism and Hinduism.

The Psalters. George Harrison. Bob Dylan's *Desolation Row*. Modern spirituals.

Defining patience as enduring pain, trouble without complaining or losing self-control. Refusing to be provoked or angered.

Patient hope?

A sense of humor helps. This morning I read of the contretemps between the Chinese government and the Dalai Lama. The Dalai Lama threatens to abort his reincarnation to deprive the Chinese government from controlling his succession. The Chinese government insists. Henceforth, the Dalai Lama will be reincarnated under Chinese auspices!

In exile I translate: Self-appointed Jewish leaders should refuse their reincarnation. Christian and

Muslim leaders, too. Or go rogue. For God's sake, do something outside state control. Refuse to enable state power.

Exiles looking back at the world, laughing out loud. For criticizing these thieves and murderers, we have been exiled? Ha!

For criticism of political leaders read the Biblical prophets. Via God, their punishment for sins: slavery, being cleansed from the land, starvation, scorched earth.

Beware of that darkness, too.

Do all things pass away? Yes, but we live in the meantime. The meantime is all we have. To be faithful.

If beyond, hope resides, how to discern if hope is real or pie in the sky?

We do not know. Hence our challenge. Martin Luther King's moral arc of the universe slowly bending toward justice. Perhaps.

Eschatological justice. Be careful what we wish for.

The prophet as agnostic about future hope. The universe may have a moral arc. It may not.

Late morning reflections in between the golden sunset and extraordinary sunrise.

Exile – living in the meantime.

◆•◆•◆

This morning, I happened onto a beach wedding and asked the couple if I could take a photo. They were happy to oblige. As I aimed my camera, the bride and groom drew close. I asked the groom to move a bit closer. Without thinking and to my surprise, I told the bride how beautiful she was. The groom thanked me. I advised him it was the bride I was complimenting. We laughed.

Truth comes by accident and from strangers. As does beauty and hope. I was surprised by my joy for the two complete strangers I happened upon by accident.

A wizened veteran of love and loss caught up by new life affirmed. As the sun rose in the sky.

In the hardship of exile. Be open to the expressions of love. Of those choosing life.

Don't look down their road as if it's your own. As if exile is everyone's fate. Forever.

◆•◆•◆

On Biblical Isaiah's eagle's wings. Perhaps. That seems a long way from where I reside. Where the world resides.

The New Jerusalem. Farther away?

The return to the Land of Israel has occurred. Failed. On this the Jewish prophetic voice is clear. Now what?

The question for the prophets in our day. All over the world. The 'Now What?' Exile. After the promise darkens.

Does the promise betrayed mean the promise was always wrong, will always be wrong, should never have been made?

◆•◆•◆•◆

A reviewer of Samuel Beckett's plays writes that Beckett discarded 'layer after layer of accidental qualities to reach the innermost core of the self.' The reviewer compared Beckett to Michelangelo who, in his sculptures, chipped away at marble to release the figure within.

As I backpacked through Italy many years ago, I was drawn to Michelangelo's unfinished sculptures. His figures emerging, as they were being born. Yet their character is already in place.

Are Beckett's plays, even taken together, unfinished? Do they probe the self's core, on route, even if they thought they were at their end?

Imagine exile as our core emerging within our unfinished prophetic journey.

Unfinished being. Unfinished journey. The core already obvious. Refusing to become stuck.

———◆•◆•◆•◆———

Exile laments. It might be better if nothing was at stake. Though I have never known such a life.

What is at stake remains or will return in this or another guise. Of course, we can miss what is at stake. False prophets and, worse, prophets without depth. Having the experience and missing the meaning.

Trying to discern what is at stake is far from easy. Even when the future appears as ominous handwriting on the wall.

———◆•◆•◆•◆———

Reading the morning newspaper. Thinking again these apparent opposites that have been on my mind for decades:

> 'History is a nightmare from which I am trying to awake.'
>
> James Joyce

> 'History is a mysterious approach to closeness.'
>
> Martin Buber

Nightmare/closeness. Intimacy within suffering? The suffering we don't want for others. The suffering we don't want for ourselves. Suffering preordained, since we live in history?

Refusing history's call is our way of deflecting intimacy. Deflecting God?

Beware of darkness.

The persistence of the prophetic.

Out of the blue, a text from my son, Isaiah. Subject: God.

Isaiah asks if I believe in God. My response: 'Complicated.' I begin to lay out the complications. His text response is immediate: 'I'm not interested in a lecture, Dad-o. Please answer my question, yes or no.'

Unprepared for a yes or no option, I buy time by retreating. I employ a distinction Isaiah offered about my fatherhood several years ago. Isaiah noted two essentials of me as father. On one hand, I am a father as usually understood, and on the other, a mentor.

I ask Isaiah if he prefers that I answer as his father or mentor. Isaiah chooses father. This makes my response easier: 'As your father, I say believe in God. Then let the conversation begin.'

Dear God,
Once again
in foreign waters
I swim dream-like
toward an unknown destination.

In foreign waters
there is no way out
As I know
only too well.

What we will be remembered for?

Does it matter?

Behind the wall of illusion we hide.

This morning before sunrise. Thoughts.

'Exiles as the canaries in the mines of the struggle for our common humanity.'

Sounds right.

'Jews of Conscience as the third rail of world empires throughout history.'

Yes.

'The exile of Jews of Conscience is permanent. Therefore humanity is on the ropes permanently.'

Quite possible.

'Exiles of all backgrounds and persuasions will come together to transform the world.'

Leap of faith.

Exile. Aftershock of the embodied prophetic.

The prophet humbled. Searching for another level. Of?

More engagement. As if the prophet is as he was. *Before?*

Engagement as necessary. Also a deflection.

Exile should not be viewed by the exiled as a learning process. Though it is.

Exile should not be viewed by the exiled as a place where more depth is achievable. Though it is.

Exile should not be viewed by the exiled as profoundly, perhaps primarily, a personal journey. Though it is.

What exiles lose. What exiles gain. Exile balance sheets. Who does the math?

Loss and gain, exiles wonder during the day, wake in the middle of the night, go through this event and that event. Over and over again.

Exile navel-gazing?

Exile interiors. Prophetic interiors. Dark corridors.

Exile, like the prophetic, persisting. The persistence of exile.

The difference between hard and soft exiles. Splitting hairs?

For those just embarking on the journey, the difference is real. Veterans of exile know.

Hard exile. When you think you cannot make it without God. When you think you cannot make it with God.

The prophetic as the wild card. Of justice. Of healing.

Imagining prophetic interiors infused with light. Instead of darkness. Both?

I have never drawn a 'Get Out of Exile Free' card. Have you?

Are the interiors of exile and the prophetic different? Since exile and the prophetic come together I think of their interiors as two-way mirrors.

Not an academic discourse here. As if exile and the prophetic are constructions. Nor shall I cite the voluminous literature on both. As if exile and the prophetic exist to be studied, analyzed or imagined.

Rather, I am thinking of duration, the persistence of exile and the prophetic in history. The persistence of both in our (real) lives as individuals. In our communities.

The prophetic as the rage for justice and meaning

in the world. Exile as the consequence of the prophetic embodied.

Exile as the day to day living of the consequences of the prophetic.

Exile as the prophetic disciplined by the powers that be.

The wounded prophetic. On its last (exile) legs.

'We are living in times that have no precedent, and in our present situation universality, which could formerly be implicit, has to be fully explicit. It has to permeate our language and the whole of our way of life.'

'A new kind of sanctity is indeed a fresh spring, an invention. If all is kept in proportion and if the order of each thing is preserved, it is almost equivalent to a new revelation of the universe and of human destiny. It is the exposure of a large portion of truth and beauty hitherto concealed under a thick layer of dust. More genius is needed than was needed by Archimedes to invent mechanics and physics. A new saintliness is a still more marvelous invention.'

Words from the French Jewish mystic, Simone Weil, to a priest, pondering her conversion to Christianity. I am drawn to the new saintliness Weil wrote about.

Yet, after many years, that 'still more marvelous invention' and 'new revelation of the universe and human destiny' eludes us.

Gone from my mind and heart. Or in retreat to return another day.

'Be careful, because if you should pass over something important through your own fault it would be a pity,' the priest admonishes Weil. Since she was intellectually acute and almost obsessive in her scruples, her priest confessor implores Weil to let unexpected thoughts and experiences resonate in her life.

Was the priest channeling the Adrienne Rich truth that often comes by accident and from strangers?

Truth, however it comes, as opportunity.

Truth, however it comes, as trauma.

The paradox of trauma. Trauma as severe injury/safe haven. Trauma as place of retreat/place of openness.

Exile ruminations. To let the unexpected arrive.

The uncertain middle of the night, sunrise hours away. A taste of eternity.

The anxiety of exile. Facing the end.

Trying prayer, if only to turn anxiety outward.

Middle of the night reading. The lives of those who are hardly considered saints in the traditional sense. Those who embody Weil's new saintliness or elements thereof.

A devourer of biographies I am, the subject's later years especially compelling. Lives being more important than time-bound words or specific events. Because witness is and isn't time-bound.

Lives lived. Mine. Ours.

Samuel Beckett writing to an admirer: 'I am flattered and touched by what you say of my work. I myself am quite incapable of talking about it. I see it and live it from the inside. There it is always dark, and in the dark no question ever of diagnosis, or prognosis, or treatment.'

Living exile from the inside. Is the dark always dark, without possibility of light?

The difficulty of talking about one's writing, analyzing or placing it before the public as a set piece. I understand this well. Beckett abjured becoming his own publicist. Feeling he would betray his very being. I understand this, too.

The prophet as a public person. Who cannot explain his interior. To others. To himself.

The prophet sees and lives the prophetic from the inside. It isn't always dark. Or rather, the dark isn't only dark.

There may be no diagnosis, prognosis or treatment, true. Yet there are moments of illumination – clarification, insight, elucidation. At least, fragments, thereof.

The Spanish Catholic priest, Joan Casañas, and his journey among guerilla fighters in Chile opposing the Pinochet regime. Inquiring as to what they, on the cutting and dangerous edge of resistance, thought about God, Casañas describes their faith as 'elucidation through abundance.'

Most of the guerillas fighters could not say God and mean it. God had been twisted by the oppressors, in politics and in the Church. The guerillas had little need for a substitute name.

To exiles like myself, a reminder: When experiencing elucidation through abundance, experience it.

Name it in the way I can. This is part of the new saintliness, at least fragments of it. I can share what I find with others.

Or is this elucidation through abundance a private experience that resists sharing?

The memory of elucidation through abundance. When elucidation through abundance flees.

Like remembering the God that. Was.

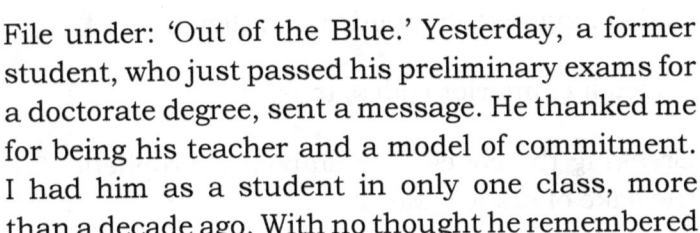

File under: 'Out of the Blue.' Yesterday, a former student, who just passed his preliminary exams for a doctorate degree, sent a message. He thanked me for being his teacher and a model of commitment. I had him as a student in only one class, more than a decade ago. With no thought he remembered me.

The impact we have on others. Keeping sight of our witness in exile. Not easy.

My student's gratitude. Expressed. A reminder. Practice and express my own.

The message of gratitude received, reflected upon, as Israel continues to oppress Palestinians. I have set aside my criticism of the ethics of Israel, wanting to reflect in other realms. Trying to deflect what cast me into exile in the first place? What keeps me here?

I couldn't help myself. So this morning I wrote. About the coded language of injustice that is periodically broken by fearmongering Jewish voters. As if the Arab world is a jungle of, so designated, 'wild beasts.'

The politics of fear. Everywhere.

The fear of exile. Everywhere.

Coded language. In politics. In religion.

Coded life. Interior codes, too?

Breaking the codes. The embodied prophetic. For the sake of justice. More.

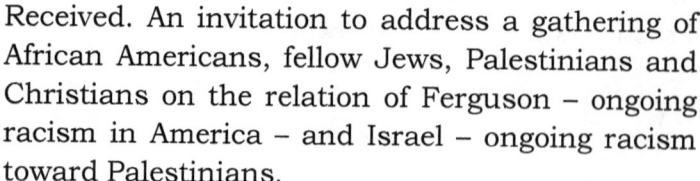

Received. An invitation to address a gathering of African Americans, fellow Jews, Palestinians and Christians on the relation of Ferguson – ongoing racism in America – and Israel – ongoing racism toward Palestinians.

The controversial, former pastor of Barack Obama, Reverend Jeremiah Wright, will be in attendance. Several rabbis, too, radical types, who have read my writing during their seminary training and beyond.

A new generation of rabbis. Who come *after* the Holocaust. And *after* Israel. The *afters* of individual and communal life, Jewish and otherwise.

Feeling respected but speaking about codes, the meeting is top secret. Only *after* will our meeting be disclosed.

Another code of silence. Fears of establishment Jews and Christians seeking to shut the venue down. Claiming it to be anti-Semitic. My, how the world turns.

Jews around every corner of my life. Empire Jews, that is.

Jews of Conscience around every corner of my life, too.

Jews on both sides of the Empire Divide.

Empire Jews. Empire Christians. Empire Muslims. Empire is interfaith.

Jews, Christians and Muslims of Conscience. Conscience is interfaith.

The absurdity of hashing out prophetic thought. In secret.

Gratitude in secret, too? Naming what is yet to be named aloud. Gratitude in the closet.

Once named, there's no going back. Never a thought about going back, if 'back' even exists.

The difficulty of locating our *befores*. Like a time before my children were born. An inaccessible foreign country.

Married to the prophetic. No before. To imagine.

The prophetic as a life-long companion. So there's no dwelling in the past or looking toward the future.

Engaged. Now. The prophetic without before or after.

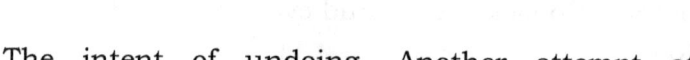

The intent of undoing. Another attempt at understanding Beckett. All of us?

This morning's sunrise. Undoing? Rewind? The first day's light of the rest of my life.

Perhaps this is where Beckett got stuck. His intent to undo. When trying to construct meaning, I get stuck, too.

Living without intent to undo or construct. Or, at least, paying attention to our efforts in both directions.

Undo self, undo God?

Constructing self, constructing God?

Self-stuck. God-stuck. Intent?

Old photos, Kodak single shot, surfacing.

At the blackboard, with chalk, writing, students listening – New York, 1981.

In a venue, seated, speaking, launching my book on a Jewish theology of liberation, respondents on either side – Jerusalem, 1987.

I am young, entering my prime.

More recent photos iPhone, group selfies included, arriving.

Seated, speaking, revisiting a Jewish theology of liberation's past for the future, the audience filled with seminarians from the Philippines, Vietnam, Malaysia, the Congo – Quezon City, 2016.

I have aged, entering my remaining years.

Nostalgia? Am glad I was. Futuristic? Am glad I am.

The prophetic strand running straight through.

Not I. Still without a clue as to where the prophetic came from.

We dwell in the abyss mouthing platitudes.

I scan the shock and outrage toward an Israeli prime minister's scandalous comments in the last hours of an Israeli election. Should the shock and outrage be less if an Israeli prime minister sweet talks the opposition?

Whatever the rhetoric, the structures of oppression continue unabated.

So true everywhere. Platitudes for every unjust occasion.

Periodic prayer. Short bursts. This morning on my foggy beach, sitting quietly. Closing my eyes.

Getting ready to travel to lecture. I anticipate lots of discussion about those who govern and enable the pursuit of Jewish empire.

Empire politicians come and go in the public spotlight. My much, much smaller public spotlight comes and goes, too.

On tour, with the others I meet, we rail against the night. Hopeless hope?

Breast milk for sale. Medicinal purposes, The *New York Times* reports. Nutrients to help with premature babies, perhaps Crohn's disease. One day.

Also becoming a booming business with monopoly and distribution issues looming. Who gets whose milk. Who doesn't.

Breast milk as a commodity. Commodification. Thought, religion and prayer (un)exempt.

Arrived in San Antonio. My Little Guy, Isaiah picks me up in my father's old car. Generations.

Dinner with a fledgling Jewish Voice for Peace chapter. Of the ten people from San Antonio present, one is Jewish. Several Palestinians. Other Muslims, too.

Mixed multitude.

Explaining the prophetic underlying Jewish dissent, my charge. For the most part, Jews don't announce themselves as prophetic or are even aware of where their voice arrives from.

Does our voice arrive from Somewhere Else?

Talk, too, of a *Yom Kippur* sermon, by a new local rabbi, Isaiah in attendance. The essence of the rabbi's message to the congregation: 'Not to worry. I'm not taking a stand on Israel. You don't have to either. Let's stand together in not taking a stand.'

Female rabbi. The change in the rabbinate needed. Hardly makes a dime's worth of difference.

Coming together for prayer. Injustice all around us. In our name. Joining the Christian club.

Membership has privileges.

Speaking the truth as I see it, gathering steam as my mini-lecture tour continues. Completely content.

To a Catholic audience, intrigue and bafflement: Can the Jewish prophetic be without God?

A conundrum.

Or are the Jewish prophets of our day simply saying no to the God they have been presented with?

A/theism.

Non-belief, skepticism, doubt. Considering the

history of affirming God. And the cycle of violence and atrocity. That such belief too often enables. Seems logical. Essential.

Enough?

❖•❖•❖•❖

The God we are presented with. The God others construct.

The God we construct. That we present to ourselves. To others.

Wrestling with their construction of God. With ours. During the day. In the middle of the night.

No exit?

❖•❖•❖•❖

PowerPoint. Showing the faces of those who embody the Jewish prophetic in our time. Twice yesterday. Once more today.

Repeating for the new audience. Repeating for myself. Their learning. My learning.

If I say what is inside of me enough times, I will learn what I know in a deeper way. Since what I know arrives within me from Somewhere Else, I have to learn even what I know. So it seems to me.

Like the prophets who do not think 'God.' As I didn't. Until the deepest exile, the one without end, came my way.

Learning God. As I speak God.

Since exile can't be understood. Wrestled with. Without God.

More lectures and discussions today, ending with a Skype session into a Chicago classroom. Discussion topic – the work of Abraham Joshua Heschel on the prophets. And my own.

During our session, my Skype-friend, professor from Brazil, Claudio, explains where Heschel and I come together and where we depart. I am all ears.

Claudio honors me. He teaches me about who I am. The definition of interfaith solidarity?

A wonderful Skype-time it was, though I was a complete failure. I couldn't define what the students wanted me to. I couldn't name God properly. I couldn't explain the prophets or the prophetic in the way that the students needed me to.

So we laughed together as I failed. Over and over again.

Later I thought: 'Those who try to sum up the prophetic through the actions of the prophet fail to understand the prophetic. Those who probe the interior of the prophets enter into deep darkness.'

When prophet-travelers return, they fumble for words. What to say about the prophetic interior to those who haven't been there?

This is what I know. No matter how deficient I am in defining the prophetic, when discussing the prophets, I am completely content. Fulfilled.

So after days of touring, I realize that my failure to define the prophetic doesn't preclude happiness. Another subject that eludes my ability to define.

Like love. God. Exile. The prophetic. The most meaningful, elusive parts of our humanity.

The prophetic as inverted poetry. Stark, explosive, loud, quiet.

On the prophetic. Images wild. Definitions elusive.

Thinking: 'Failure for those who try to sum up the prophetic exterior. Darkness for those who probe the prophetic interior.'

The prophets – also – content? Happy? The Bible doesn't let us in on the prophetic interior too often. When it does, contentment and happiness aren't apt descriptions. Far from it.

Better, paired, descriptions of the Biblical prophets: driven/despair, power/weakness, rescue by God/abandoned by God, illuminated mission/doomed mission, deep darkness/glimmers of light.

The pairings can be reversed; in the Bible, they are often rearranged and recycled. The Biblical prophets are iconic/inconclusive. Based on the evidence, the take-away of the ordinary reader of the Bible: It's better if someone else receives the prophetic call.

Think of the Biblical prophetic as a deeply troubling but fascinating movie you watch, sit for a while as the credits roll and then leave the theatre. So nice to be away from ordinary life for a couple of hours. Nice, also, to return to ordinary life.

Albert Camus's Sisyphus. Rolling his boulder up and down the mountain. Condemned by the Gods to a life without forward movement, his only solace being consciousness of his fate. Camus imagines Sisyphus happy.

The prophet. Condemned (by God?) to a life of exile without respite. Her only solace being consciousness of her calling. Would Camus imagine the prophet happy?

———◆·◆·◆·◆———

Happy as in blessed, blissful, bright, golden, halcyon, prosperous. Derivations thereof.

Inverted happiness?

CliffsNotes : Camus on Sisyphus:

'Camus concludes his essay by arguing that happiness and absurd awareness are intimately connected. We can only be truly happy, he suggests, when we accept our life and our fate as entirely our own—as the only thing we have and as the only thing we will ever be. The final sentence reads: 'One must imagine Sisyphus happy.' But why *must* we imagine Sisyphus happy? Camus's wording suggests that we have no choice in the matter. But is there an alternative? Sisyphus is the absurd hero, the man who loved life so much that he has been condemned to an eternity of futile and hopeless labor. And yet he is above that fate precisely because he is aware of it. If Sisyphus is not happy in this awareness, then absurd awareness does not bring happiness. It would then follow that happiness is only possible if we evade absurd awareness, if we leap into hope or faith.'

Transposed for the prophetic, what can I make of this?

Accepting our life and fate as our own, as the only thing we have and the only thing we will ever be. Avoiding the leap into a hope or faith that solves the immense riddle of the prophetic.

Embracing the prophetic, aware of our futile and hopeless labor.

The Absurd Prophetic. Accepting our life and our fate as the only thing we have and the only thing we will ever be.

No Exit Prophetic. Leading to No Exit Exile. Rolling the prophetic boulder up the mountain of injustice. The meaning of the prophetic, found in moments of reflection. Our consciousness of the prophetic being what we have.

Is happiness achievable with this awareness?

Camus, my first love. *The Myth of Sisyphus*, an absurd happiness. *The Rebel*, the rebellion against injustice.

Not enough though. I couldn't stay there. The prophetic was too deep. The prophetic, even then, finding its way through. The prophetic being more, yes, but without transcending Camus's understandings. As if the prophetic is an answer to Camus's insufficiency.

The prophetic isn't an answer. To Sisyphus. To the rebel. To anything.

The prophetic isn't an answer to the absurdity of life. Or the failure of rebellion. The prophetic recognizes both. Enhanced.

The Apostle Paul, another angle. Seeing through a glass darkly. The prophet is in over her head, too. Like Sisyphus, the prophet knows only in part.

One day, I shall come face to face and know even as I am known. Doubtful.

The (un)knowing of the prophet. Dark interiors. The (un)knowing of all of us. The prophet within.

Walking with our (un)knowing. Is there any other choice? Those who know everything hardly know much. Those who know little. Know enough. To take a stand.

Knowing what we need to know. Not less. Not more. Taking it on the road. The embodied prophetic.

(Un)knowing even more than we already (un)know.

Deconstructing our (un)knowing. Of ourselves. Of the prophetic. Of God.

Deconstructing until we hit the core. Of our (un)knowing.

The Cloud of Unknowing, the spiritual guide. Brought back to prophetic earth.

A response to my (un)knowing: 'Samuel Johnson's Prince Rasselas travels the world looking for happiness and it finally brings him back to where he started.'

Is the only happiness possible for the prophet to return to a familiar place and to know it – really – for the first time?

To know or to embrace the prophetic. Perhaps the same thing. Or perhaps two different movements, one leading to the other, the other leading back.

The prophetic is Something Other than linear.

Sisyphus's mountain is one of many mountains the prophets climb.

The geography of the prophet is focused and wide-ranging. Intense awareness. Compassion, too. Awareness embodied. In the life of others who are suffering.

After the public expression, that rage against injustice and hypocrisy, the prophet experiences an inner depression. The dark interiors of the prophetic endure, loom large, without illumination.

The public airing of the prophet's lament does not rescue the prophet from the deepest of exiles.

No exit from exile. Rescue only in the literary imagination. Is this true of Sisyphus, too?

A failure last night, my last lecture of the tour. I spent an hour circling around the prophetic.

Is there a prophetic stance regarding Israel, as in a solution to the Israel-Palestine conflict, that would be prophetically correct?

The prophetic isn't about solutions. Since if anything is resolved anywhere the prophet is already on the move toward the next crisis point. Somewhere, the prophetic voice is always needed.

But the Jewish prophetic isn't moving on from here. The Jewish prophetic has come full circle. First within Jewish life, then outward toward the Other Nations, now returning to its indigenous interior.

The Jewish prophetic within. Whatever the outcome of Israel-Palestine, even against the odds, the ethical rupture is already too great. Unrepairable.

Tikkun Olam. Repairing the tear in the ethical universe. From the Holocaust. From Jewish violence toward Palestinians. No.

The tear that will not mend even as the world moves on. Another challenge for the embattled Jewish prophetic.

Yesterday morning Isaiah came for breakfast. Standing together we recited the prayer I've missed.

Today I recited the prayer myself.

Different.

Leaving for home today. After breakfast this morning with Isaiah, we recited our last prayer together – for now.

Naming the world in public. Naming my interior world. Disjunction. Dissonance. Search for the connection. Bridge.

Ezekiel's surprise – the doom-laden text God commands him to eat tastes sweet. Speaking on the prophetic, encountering the prophetic once again, this week was sweet. With dark corners.

Easter coming around. Passover, too. I identify more with Jesus's Passion than the Exodus liberation. This, as a Jew.

Passion without resurrection, that is. Exile without rescue. Nonetheless, thanking God for making me, and my children, Jews.

Another dissonance. More than cognitive.

Remembering Gillian Rose, the late British Jewish philosopher. Known to my tour host, Judith, who years ago sat in on Gillian's class on Hegel, the great German philosopher. I sat in her class once, too. Without understanding a word she said. When I told Gillian that she was speaking over my head, she remarked to a friend sitting nearby that I was a 'charmer.' Imagine that.

I first met Gillian on a delegation to Auschwitz. When I carried her bag into the hotel, I noticed her shoelaces were untied. Without thinking, I bent down and tied them.

Soon after our time at Auschwitz, Gillian became ill. On her deathbed, she converted to Christianity. I wrote a remembrance of her for the *Tablet* in London. I placed her within the folds of Jewish history.

Gillian would have been 'charmed' by being so placed.

These Jewish women. Gillian reminded me of Simone Weil.

I loved Gillian. Still do.

Imagining myself happy. And loved. As I arrived home, I once again thought of this possibility. Happy – with all its baggage, including love. The happiness that makes sense in our lives.

Prayer that makes sense in our lives. If it does.

Jewish that makes sense in our lives.

Love that makes sense in our lives.

God that makes sense in our lives.

Wanting more or less than what makes sense won't cut it.

Exile prayer Jewish love God = happiness?

Not simple. Not out of reach.

The Jewish prison, from which Jean Daniel, the French writer, wants to escape. The prison that I, too, inhabit. Without wanting to be released.

Daniel wants to be human – only. As others are. Since he doesn't believe in God. Or anything ethnically Jewish. He is tired of being reminded by other Jews that there is no escape from being Jewish. And being reminded by non-Jews, too. Thus, Daniel's prison metaphor.

I met Daniel in Geneva some years ago. Both of us were speaking after an earlier Israeli decimation of Gaza. 'Not in our name,' he said.

Not in our name, we prisoners, being Jewish.

The prison which is Jewish. Call it what you want. Onerous at times. Also the birthplace of the prophetic. You cannot have one without the other.

Add exile to the mix. The Jewish brew. *Par excellence.*

I need another name for the cauldron that births and refines the prophetic voice. If I am able to imagine the prophet happy.

Turn the prison inside out. Somehow. If I am to continue thanking God for creating me a Jew and calling me to be free.

'Some things take so long but how do I explain.' – George Harrison

Feeling that over the last days. The inability to explain my interior. Our interiors. Living in between others. In between ourselves.

Trying to explain what we do not know. Or, worse, what we know. What takes so long doesn't necessarily become clearer. Or more articulate.

With age some things become clearer, other things less so. Like the prophetic, clarity is rarely a straight shot.

The anniversary of Oscar Romero's death, now officially declared a saint. Dying for his faith. In humanity? Rising in the history of the Salvadoran people. For a renewed humanity?

I spoke about Romero a few years ago during a meeting with a group of clergy who are scared to death of Jewishness, the local rabbi and being called anti-Semites. Perhaps they are scared to death they might be anti-Semitic, despite their training and best intentions.

Ambivalence about Jews is the coin of the Christian realm. Admit it. Then get on with an encounter of reconciliation that has depth.

Anxiety about Jews comes when Christians are called on the carpet by the local Jewish community. Here, it is represented by the rabbi of congregation *Beth El* – in Hebrew, House of God. I call it *Temple Beth Enabling Occupation.*

The clergy listened intently. I suggested a way out. Invite a Jewish Voice for Peace rabbi to their congregation and, being a welcoming congregation, invite the local rabbi to join the fun!

Through Romero, I first imagined resurrection as possible for me. Should I imagine meeting Romero when I rise in the history of the Jewish people?

Will Romero, as Paul entreated his resurrection brothers and sisters, greet me by name?

Scattered thoughts. Half prayers.

Forgetting to give back. The beauty that surrounds us. How we break each other's heart. Causing so much pain.

The clock winds down. Prayers that go nowhere.

Kairos. Seizing the moment. Time *after.*

Isaiah's shelter from the storm.

Awoke from a terrible dream. My family and I were stranded on an island soon to be obliterated by an extreme weather event. An end of the world affair. I searched for my children so we could die together.

I woke myself up and changed the pace. Surfing through my Facebook feed, I found a preview of a Palm Sunday sermon by a minister friend living in Jerusalem. She's thinking themes and asks me for my take on it.

Then reading an article posted in the Jewish *Forward* featuring the most popular Passover narratives on Amazon.

My friend's sermon imagined Jesus's entry into Israeli occupied Jerusalem. What would Jesus do? Yes, without a mention of what Jesus, at least those who bless his name, have done.

In the most popular Passover stories, Palestinians are absent. The message: Why ruin such a festive occasion?

So should I respond to my friend's request? I think celebrating a renewed Christianity as if Christianity transcends its history. As if Christianity, even in its modern formation, is innocent. Doesn't work.

Too, celebrating Jewish liberation as if we are not oppressing another people. As if our modern 'redemption' is innocent. Doesn't work either.

Our holy days aren't innocent. Now what?

Our Biblical entry into the land. Jesus's entry into Jerusalem. Powerful. Mythic. Apocryphal.

The modern Jewish entry into the land to carve the state of Israel out of Palestine. The Jewish occupation of Palestine. Powerful. Mythic. Real.

The clash between apocryphal and real. Highlighted or buried during Easter and Passover.

Mostly buried.

Middle of the night. Awakening from another nightmare. Rereading Thomas Merton's *Asian Journal*. Merton quoting Milarepa, a Tibetan Buddhist monk from many centuries ago: 'It is the tradition of the fortunate seekers never to be content with partial practice.'

Food for Passover thought.

A liberation that oppresses another people. Partial practice, if that.

Overcoming Passover. As prepackaged for us today. Refusing to be content.

Becoming one of the fortunate seekers. A tradition worth belonging to.

Bearing the costs of overcoming.

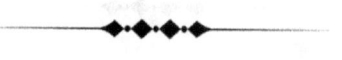

Our salvation cannot be found in the oppression of the Other.

Our liberation cannot be found in the oppression of the Other.

If our salvation is dependent on the oppression of Other, it cannot be our salvation.

If our liberation is dependent on the oppression of the Other, it cannot be our liberation.

Salvation/liberation as the great reversal, always moving outward. Toward those who suffer.

Solidarity as the movement of the heart, mind and body toward those who are suffering. Too often because of the supposedly saved and liberated.

'Saved' and 'liberated' should be reserved for those who suffer. The saved and liberated.

Refuse Easter and Passover for the well-heeled. Even those with the best of intentions.

Milarepa's 'tradition of fortunate seekers.' Though it often appears to be the case, we are rarely alone in the struggle to overcome partial practice.

When we practice exile together we are more than our individual selves. Companions on the journey.

Mostly an imagined community, true. Sometimes real.

Be open to the imagined and the real.

Passover/Easter. Deliverance by God. Not only.

On the one hand, Passover/Easter is too often celebrated to assuage our trauma of injustice. Protecting us from the injustice we benefit from.

On the other hand, Passover/Easter is sometimes used to struggle against the final assimilation to unjust power. Protecting us from the ultimate sin of idolatry.

Interesting how both are so easily assimilated to power. Holy days, with their festivities, gilded with affluence and power.

Passover/Easter. With or without God. Defining us. Can we deliver ourselves?

Our struggle to overcome partial practice. Continuing. Can we overcome partial practice without God?

Deconstructing Passover. Deconstructing Easter. The stories we recite are constructed through a Biblical filter. Without confusing the stories with a history that is shrouded in antiquity.

Did the Exodus happen? Historians aren't sure. Jesus's life, death and resurrection. Without historical verification.

I have never seen a bush on fire that left to burn was not consumed. Nonetheless the image remains deep inside my being.

It is hard to believe in a savior in a still unredeemed world and whose many followers make a future redeemed world difficult to contemplate. Count me an agnostic leaning toward atheism on this one. Too much pie in the sky, historically and in the present, used to justify oppression.

An Easter slap on Jews. Take that for disbelieving the resurrection of the Lord!

A Passover slap on Palestinians. Take that for disbelieving God gave us the land!

LOL. If the suffering wasn't so intense. Ongoing. Enabled. Praised.

◆•◆•◆•◆

Exile and the prophetic commences with the Exodus story. The rabbinic interpretations are commentary. Sometimes illuminating. Also used to discipline and disenfranchise the prophetic.

The Exodus is unproven historically. The prophets, though, are historically verifiable over time. The Exodus was a one-off event. The prophetic persists. It is exploding again in our time.

Our Passover moment has arrived. The Ten Plagues of Israeli occupation.

The persistence of the Exodus through the prophets. Who keep on arriving.

Strange. Of the Easter season sermons I am reading, the progressive ones, from Jerusalem and elsewhere, Jesus is imagined as confronting injustice. Yet to come across one that identifies Jesus as a Jew or emphasizes Jesus's Jewishness, recently in vogue, is rare.

Jews, having been denigrated, after the Holocaust, were prized. Christianity could be reclaimed from its own sins. Now the violence Jews are perpetrating makes the Jewishness of Jesus inconvenient. Those Christians who continue to claim Jesus as a Jew romanticize Jews for their own benefit. Yet another deflection.

Conundrum. Christians using Jews. Christians sidelining Jews. Do Jews exist for Christian use?

In the materialist reading of the New Testament, the Jewish Jesus confronts the occupying powers of his day, the Romans and the Jewish establishment. Today, as a Jew, Jesus would confront the occupying powers of our day, Jewish Israelis and their Jewish enablers far and wide. As a Jew.

If you hesitate to call Jesus a Jew, do you call him a Christian? After all, the prophetic Jesus didn't materialize out of thin air.

Jesus materialized out of Jewish air.

For God's sake, tell it like it is.

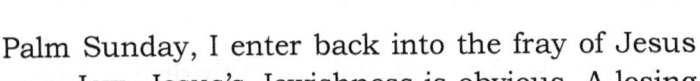

Palm Sunday, I enter back into the fray of Jesus as a Jew. Jesus's Jewishness is obvious. A losing battle, though. Probably not worth fighting.

Having a Jewish savior isn't easy. Especially if you are a Palestinian Christian. The deep ambivalence about Jews plays a part for others, too. If you see your Christian faith as singular, dependence on those you have supposedly replaced can only be a bummer.

That's the thing about Jews. We are still hanging around. On the move for good and ill.

The different faces of religion. Religion highlights humanity's depth. Dumbs down thought, too. Religion's vocation: taming the prophetic?

Why travel back into old entanglements that rarely go anywhere?

Standing on principle regardless. The need to have my say.

Passover/Easter brings out the best and worst of all of us.

My yearly Passover plea for justice. One more despairing than the other. To no avail. Our ethical abyss deepens by the day. I should let it pass this year.

Passover as irrelevant. Will it simply disappear?

Writing my Passover plea anyway.

Calling out Christians of Conscience who portray Jesus as a prophetic figure who resists occupation. Excluding Jesus's Jewishness.

Calling out Jews who portray the Exodus as a gift to the world that keeps on giving Israel. Without decrying the continuing oppression of Palestinians.

Expressing myself. To an audience so small it hardly adds up.

Am I a voice in the wilderness of my own making?

Our voices, too. In the wilderness. Our audience so small.

------◆·◆·◆·◆------

'The contemplative life must provide an area, a space of liberty, of silence in which possibilities are allowed to surface and new choices – beyond routine choice – become manifest. It should create a new experience of time, not as a stop-gap, stillness, but as *temps vierge* – not a blank to be filled or an untouched space to be conquered and violated, but a space which can enjoy its own potentialities and hopes – and its own presence to itself. One's *own* time. But not dominated by one's ego and its demands. Hence open to others – *compassionate time*, rooted in the sense of common illusion and in criticism of it.'

Many years ago I highlighted this passage from Thomas Merton's *Asian Journal*. Hinting at the silence within the prophetic. But what is the 'common illusion and in criticism of it?' How can compassionate time be thus rooted?

Rereading Merton's diaries. As they were, uncensored. My attraction to Merton.

Are the prophets also monks?

Easter approaching. The theme of resurrection as a form of hope is everywhere. I am agnostic on this hope; if truth be told, an atheist.

Christianity is bound up with resurrection hope. In my mind, Christianity should move toward the unadorned prophetic. Without hope. Without rescue. Where speech about God is barely possible. Or in hushed voices only. Like disclosing a closely guarded secret.

Written in prison, before his execution, Dietrich Bonhoeffer's 'arcane discipline.' Split wide open.

Bonhoeffer's sense that God was no longer necessary to explain our world was right. But the corollary, that humanity had 'come of age,' was wrong. At least, debatable. Perhaps unsustainable.

Coming of age, knowing science and developing technology, is one side of progress. The other side, mass dislocation and death.

Arcane – mysterious, secret, hidden, deep. Impenetrable?

Discipline – instruction, knowledge, rigor, renunciation. Fidelity?

Passover liberation, as a form of hope, is like Easter hope, the easy way out. Where there is none.

Avoid the Passover/Easter hoopla. Like the plague.

Note where 'Next Year in Jerusalem' – in its various manifestations – leads.

To be a religious person is not about hope. Not even close.

Sent two quotes by a friend without commentary. Related to my sense that a religious person isn't about hope.

'If they give you ruled paper, write the other way.'
– Juan Ramón Jiménez

'When we are not sure, we are alive.'
– Graham Greene

Passover and Easter have become religious container boxes where our hope is (dis)placed. For safekeeping. Until next year.

So during the run-up to both holidays I write and pray the other way.

Pray the other way. To where I am not sure. Suggestions?

At least I should get on the dissenting religious bandwagon with progressives who rearrange the deck chairs of our sinking ship. To reinvent their particular religion as if it is innocent.

If only for strategic reasons. Everyone needs company.

But the interfaith gatherings, with everyone in their religious costumes, drives me crazy.

How many on the religious bandwagon are there for strategic reasons? Or to assuage their impossible religious affiliations?

The disappointments grow. Even our radical deconstructionists can be careerists.

Pre-Passover/Easter depression. Hope that my sunrise beach walk helps.

The colors of the sky and ocean, my renewal. In a world without rescue. Life.

Though I am not celebrating Passover, because we are permanently oppressing another people, I went to the grocery store to buy *matzah*. When I couldn't find any on the shelf, I asked a grocery clerk: 'In the Ethnic Foods section, Sir.'

I chuckled. Jews as an ethnic group. A far cry from Biblical chosenness. The American, modern, slippery slope.

Add our own slippery slope. Oppressing another people.

Such are my Passover thoughts.

I left the Ethnic Foods section without buying *matzah*. Instead, I will bake my own like I did last year. With the understanding that I am not celebrating Passover. No way.

Bit rusty on the *matzah*. Will try again tonight. As the cascade of Easter images continue.

Yesterday, the checkout woman at the grocery store handed me the receipt and wished me Happy Easter. Wearing bunny ears.

My conclusion? Easter is endless in the land of empire and no doubt elsewhere as well. Like Christmas. No rescue from either.

Now there are objections to my posting about an outrageous, anti-Zionist Jewish Israeli who everyone, including Palestinians, refuse to work with. The issue is that his criticism of Israel is so strong it evokes anti-Semitism. That he is a self-hating Jew. Everyone wants distance from him.

But, thinking, have they ever gone into the weeds of the Biblical prophetic? Few do anymore.

Jews and others who invoke the prophets usually mine a couple of Biblical verses calling for universal justice. Exile and the costs to the people Israel – slavery, rape, death on a large scale, all envisioned with incredibly vivid imagery – are left out.

If you mine the prophets for a heart of gold, watch out, you will find some very disturbing nightmare visions. The Biblical prophets make the Israeli Jew I refer to, as others like him, seem like a piece of cake, a walk in the park.

Add any other cliché that softens the rough edges of our Jewish inheritance. After a while it becomes a habit. Can the Biblical prophets be read today without cliché?

Yes, too, the deconstruction of the prophetic rough edges by those who find the prophets patriarchal, prone to sweeping condemnations and alike. Which they certainly are.

Without the rough edges of the prophets, however, prophetically-speaking, what will we be left with? Passover bunny ears?

Yesterday. Easter. On my daily sunrise walk I happen on to a sunrise service. Easter deluxe.

Evangelical in tone. Hymns through loudspeakers. The Atoning Blood.

Overcast sky. Will it rain on the worshippers?

Amidst dark clouds, the sun begins to rise. The congregation is seated on beach chairs. I'm offered a pamphlet which I take. I'm offered grape juice and bread in a plastic container. I politely decline.

I take photographs. As an observer. The music is getting louder. More Atoning Blood.

Did Jesus die for me?

The day after the Easter Rising, junk on the beach. From Easter vacationers. Worshippers, too.

Bottles, wrappers, you name it. The beach is full of trash.

Trash doesn't rise. Our (still) unredeemed world.

Troubling it is. What we want of life, what we are in life. The distance is great.

Religion – to bring what God wants us to be, what we are, into closer proximity. Does it?

Shunryu Suzuki: "For Zen students a weed is a treasure."

Yes and rereading this during Passover, in exile, and in exile from Passover, too, a reminder of placing too much emphasis on Big Things. They often ring hollow.

Weeds are always of interest when we arrive at the prophetic. But even then we can get stuck on their relation to Big Things and their underbelly.

Turned upside down and around weeds have a life of their own. And a sometimes unexpected beauty.

Pay attention to the small things. Mindful. Of what is here. Not trying to solve the Big Things.

That will not be solved.

The prophetic is a Big Thing. Would it be better if the prophetic had never emerged?

Dereliction of duty. Another (prophetic) Big Thing.

Big Passover. Big Easter. Don't go far. Anywhere, really. All the hoopla, then tucked away for next year. The next year Big Thing.

What to do if the Big Thing you have been working on your whole life isn't really what religion is made it out to be. Or, thinking of the justice map, isn't going anywhere?

Faith, too, if you want to separate it from religion. How is that going?

What you thought religion, justice, faith to be. Or made them to be. In our own likeness.

Suzuki: 'In the beginner's mind there are many possibilities, but in the expert's there are few.'

Beginner's mind. The prophetic eviscerated. Or thought anew?

The prophetic, by definition, involved with the Big Thing. Time to begin again?

Suzuki: 'Usually when someone believes in a particular religion, his attitude becomes more and more a sharp angle pointing away from himself. In our way the point of the angle is always toward ourselves.'

Pointing the prophetic toward ourselves. Rather than a sharp angle pointing away. Is this surrender on the field of battle?

The rumblings of history. God in history. AWOL. The sharp angle of the prophetic pointing toward ourselves, the people Israel. Is that, in another way, pointing away?

Temptations around every corner. Even the prophets sometimes need beginner's mind.

Sunrise. Open sky except for a few scattered dark clouds. Then light on the horizon.

Imagining the prophetic as the interplay of darkness and light.

Reimagining the prophetic. Passover fading.

Franz Kafka's diary: 'All is imaginary – family, office, friends, the street – all imaginary, far way or close at hand, the woman closest of all, but the truth is only that you are pressing your head against the wall of a windowless and doorless cell.'

Of this, Kafka's biographer writes: 'Kafka was standing at the threshold of the world of Samuel Beckett, unprepared to endure it. He would eschew this image from then on, as though it had scorched him. He turned back and charted another course of his own.'

Scorched. Exile and the prophetic. Our heads against the wall. We need to find a window and a door.

We?

Charting my own course. Beginning again.

Finding my window. My door. Someone else's won't do.

Kafka is instructive. When there is no way forward, look again. For light. An opening. There for everyone. In our own way.

When the Big Thing is exposed. As less than you thought. Or way too much. Go small.

Keeping my Passover head above water as the last days approach. My homemade *matzah* – with black currants – is almost perfected.

Ritual *matzah*. Without the meaning. Like praying to God. Without God.

Nonetheless kept.

As Passover breathes its last breath. The alternative is nothingness. Another ritual.

Merton's last journal entries before he dies. Thinking he had almost squandered his vocation. Now back on the last legs of life, in full form, his deep solitude shared fully with others.

As Merton shared his solitude with his Asian compatriots, they shared their solitude with him.

Shared solitude. Until it becomes more?

Sharing our solitude. Beyond the Big Thing.

Passover is over. Easter, too. We return to our everyday lives of work, love and failure.

Without guide or rescue. Just life.

Dylan's 'life and life only.' Worth living?

Deflation is hard. Just life. Not going anywhere. Really.

The illusion of the swinging *I* door. Until that *I* door no longer swings.

The exile *I*. Disappearing?

The prophetic *I*. In history?

The suffering *I*. Illusion?

The great encounter. Exile/prophetic/suffering. Does Buddhism have that covered?

Writing against the religious calendar. That elevates and sometimes clouds our vision. Of life on earth. As we have it.

If there wasn't a religious calendar to write against, we would have to invent one.

I have seen the 'no incense' secular folks. Witnessed their gains and losses from the front row. There is a secular abyss, too.

Filled with all sorts of Gods. Many.

Our religious Gods. Our secular Gods. Where is God when we need God most?

Perhaps we have misplaced our need. Misplaced God?

We are on our own, it seems, to think about, to experience. Our loss and gain.

The God That Was. Aren't we already here. At the end of things? Looking at the wonderful sky, at young lovers in their prime, at our children growing tall.

As we age.

Knowing, somewhere, deep inside. That there is enough left. To begin again.

www.ingramcontent.com/pod-product-compliance
Lightning Source LLC
Chambersburg PA
CBHW060915190426
43197CB00012BA/2496